Contents

KT-161-302

LEARNING RESOURCE CENTRE
READING COLLEGE AND SCHOOL OF ART & DESIGN
KINGS ROAD, READING RG1 4HJ
0118 967 5060

Return on or before the last date stamped below.

Linford Christie

Published in association with The Basic Skills Agency

Hodder & Stoughton

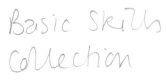

Acknowledgements
Cover: © *Empics*
Photos: p. 2 © *Empics; p. 6* © *Action Images; pp. 8, 22* © *Colorsport; p. 11* © *Allsport; p. 16* © *Action Plus; pp. 21, 27* © *PA.*

Orders: please contact Bookpoint Ltd, 130 Milton Park, Abingdon, Oxon OX14 4SB. Telephone: (44) 01235 827720, Fax: (44) 01235 400454. Lines are open from 9.00 – 6.00, Monday to Saturday, with a 24 hour message answering service. Email address: orders@bookpoint.co.uk

British Library Cataloguing in Publication Data
A catalogue record for this title is available from The British Library

ISBN 0 340 84878 2

Second edition. First published 1994.
Impression number   10 9 8 7 6 5 4 3 2 1
Year   2007 2006 2005 2004 2003 2002

Typeset by SX Composing DTP, Rayleigh, Essex.
Printed in Great Britain for Hodder & Stoughton Educational, a division of Hodder Headline Plc, 338 Euston Road, London NW1 3BH by The Bath Press Ltd.

1   Early Life

Linford was born
in St Andrews, Jamaica
in April 1960.

He came to London
when he was seven.

He had lots of jobs –
tax collector, social worker, bank clerk –
before he got serious
about his running.

He did not train at all
until he was 20.
Like a lot of young people,
he liked staying up late,
going to clubs and parties.

Linford started training when he was 20.

2 Winning

In August 1993,
Linford Christie
won a gold medal
in the 100 metres
at the World Championships
in Stuttgart, Germany.

Now he had won gold
in all the big races:
the Commonwealth Games,
the European Games,
the Olympic Games
and now the World Championships.

After the race, Linford said,
'I think I've gone beyond
being just the greatest British athlete.

'I should be up there somewhere
among the greatest athletes of all time.'

3   In Trouble

Linford has had his share of trouble.
He is always in the news.

At the Olympic Games
in Seoul, in Korea,
he was suspected of taking drugs.
His drugs test was positive.
But he got off without a ban.

Once he was arrested in London,
suspected of stealing a car.
In fact, it was on loan
from a friend.

Linford sued the police,
and won £30,000.

Linford has also been in trouble
for not paying money
to the mothers of his children.

(Yvonne Oliver gave birth to Linford's twins,
Korel and Liam, in 1988.
And Judith Osborne had Linford's son,
called Merrick, in 1980.)

But Linford took the *Sun* newspaper to court
when it printed this story about his children.
He said it wasn't true.
And Linford won.

Linford always speaks his mind.

In 1992,
he led a boycott against South Africa.

He said that black athletes would not run
in South Africa
until things changed there
for black people.

Linford won a gold medal at the 1992 Olympics in Barcelona.

4 Rivals

On the track, one big rival
was the American, Leroy Burrell.
After one race,
Linford said he would kill Burrell.

Another big rival
was another American, Carl Lewis.

Linford's best-ever 100 metre run
was 9.87 seconds.
This is just one hundredth of a second slower
than Lewis's world record run of 9.86 seconds.

But some people think
that Lewis had help from a following wind
on the day he ran,
and that Linford is really faster.

In Gateshead, in July 1993,
Linford beat Carl Lewis.

Linford beating Carl Lewis (left) at Gateshead in 1993.

5 Big Business

Linford and Carl Lewis
got £100,000 each
for the race in Gateshead –
not bad for ten seconds of work!

Linford also won a Mercedes car
when he won the World Championship.

The sports company Puma
paid him millions of pounds
to wear their sports shoes.

Linford set up his own company,
called Nuff Respect,
to look after the business side of his career.

Nuff Respect shows that
Linford has got a head for business.
It also shows that he thinks about his future.

6   Back on Track

In February 1995,
Linford added two more World Records
to his collection.
They were the World Indoor 60 metres record,
and the World Indoor 20 metres record.

He ran the 60 metres in 6.47 seconds,
and the 200 metres in 20.25 seconds.

In 1994, Linford's old rival, Leroy Burrell,
had shaved a hundredth of a second
off the 100 metres world record.
He ran it in 9.85 seconds.

But Linford stayed at the top longer
than Burrell or Carl Lewis.

Linford running against his rival, Leroy Burrell.

Linford's next big rival
was Donovan Bailey.
He was born in Jamaica,
but ran for Canada.

He was a friend of Linford,
as well as a rival
on the track.

Bailey beat Linford in August 1995,
and took his world title from him.
This was in Gothenburg,
in Sweden.

Linford had a hamstring injury.
He said: 'I am running in pain
that I could do without.'

7   'I Can't Go On'

It was a difficult time for Linford
between 1994 and 1995.
His injuries would not go away.

One day he would drop out of a race,
because of injury.
The next week, he would run in a race,
and beat everyone
with a world record time!
He just couldn't settle down to winning every race.

Then Linford got into a long dispute
with the British Athletics Federation.
He said he wanted more money to race.
They said they'd go bankrupt
if they paid him what he wanted.

The B.A.F. stopped him running in some top races
until the dispute was settled.

Linford gets very angry with the media,
especially when they suggest he's getting old
and he should retire.
He thinks he doesn't get enough respect
from the media.

In June 1995, Linford went on live TV.
He was under a lot of stress and
he was near to tears.

He said he would not be running
in the 1996 Olympics in Atlanta, USA.

'I just can't take any more,'
he said, 'I just can't.
I wake up every day,
and I don't know if I can go on.'

Two days later, Linford's mother,
Mabel Christie, died.
She was 65,
and had been ill for some time.

Linford flew back to Britain,
and called off another race.

8   Will he, Won't he?

Linford kept saying he would not run
in the 1996 Olympics in Atlanta.

'Gothenburg was my last championship.
I could happily stop now,' he said.
'I know I've achieved everything.
I don't think the public could love me more
than they do now.'

But would his fans let him retire before Atlanta?
Could they talk him into running one more race?

Would Linford run in another Olympic final,
at the grand old age of 36?
Could he add one more gold medal
to his collection?

Donovan Bailey winning the 100m final in Gothenburg.

The Canadian Donovan Bailey,
a great friend of Linford's,
knew the answer:
'Ask any sprinter in the world,
and he'll tell you Linford will be there.'

He was right.
Linford did go to Atlanta.
He was Men's Team Captain again.
And he did get to the final of the men's 100 metres.

But Donovan Bailey could not know
how the race would go,
or how Linford would bow out
of his last big race.

9   **Atlanta**

When Linford got to the final,
he knew that other runners had been faster
in the early races.

He knew he needed a good start.
His best runs always have good starts –
he says he goes on the B of BANG!

But this time he went too early.
False start.
Linford waved a hand to say – yes it was me.
The sprinters all had to come back,
settle down, and start again.

But then – another false start.

This time it was another runner, Ato Boldon,
who got the blame.
He was in lane 3, next to Linford.

Boldon did not think he was to blame.
He was angry,
everyone was nervous.
They all had to settle down and try again.

For the third time,
the gun went to start the race,
then went again to stop the runners –
another false start!

Linford couldn't believe it.
The judges were saying it was him!
Linford thought he had had a good start.
He thought he had gone on the B of BANG.
But the official clock told a different story.

Athletes take a tenth of a second
to react to the starter's gun.
But Linford had reacted in only 0.086 of a second.

It meant that he had jumped the gun.
He was a hundredth of a second too early.

The rules say two false starts, and you're out.

Linford running in a qualifying heat in Atlanta.

But Linford refused to go.

He didn't believe he was in the wrong,
so he threw the red flag
from his starting blocks,
argued with officials,
and held up the race for seven minutes.

Then he threw his running shoes in a rubbish bin,
and walked from the race track.

In the end the race went ahead without him.

His old friend and rival
Donovan Bailey,
won the race.

And it was a new World Record – 9.84 seconds!

Linford refuses to comment to reporters after his disqualification at Atlanta.

10 After Atlanta

After the race,
there were lots of comments about Linford.
Not all of them were good.

The newspapers,
who had fallen out with Linford before,
came back to rubbish him again.

The *Sun's* headline was
LINFORD DIDN'T SHOW 'NUFF RESPECT.

And some of the runners said
Linford's protests messed up the race.
It broke their concentration
and spoiled their chance of a medal.

But Linford said:
'I still think I got a perfect start . . .
I went with the gun.

'I was well within my rights to protest.
My Olympic title was on the line.'

Did the Atlanta crowds
think Linford was a bad sport?

'No,' said Linford.
'I was robbed and the crowd was robbed . . .
They were booing all the judges.'

But as Olympic Team Captain,
Linford didn't let things get him down.

'I'm a big rubber ball,' he said.
'I'll bounce back.'

'I lost my Olympic title today.
But I can't say I was beaten.'

But Linford was beaten, fair and square,
in Sheffield in August 1996,
by a young Scottish sprinter
called Ian Mackie.

Linford said he was going to retire.
He was 36.

'I achieved everything I set out to do,'
he said.
'I retired with ten gold medals.'

Linford began to coach young athletes.
They were all champions in the making,
all the stars of the next generation.

But he didn't stay out of trouble for long.

In February 1999,
Linford tested positive for nandrolone.

Nandrolone is a banned drug.
Yet you can pick up traces of it
from power drinks
and other food supplements,
even from some cold cures.

Linford was angry.
'I don't agree with drugs,'
he said.
'I've never taken drugs
to improve my performance.
I'll take a lie detector to prove it!'

But Linford was banned from athletics
for two years.

He had to stop
some of his coaching work.
And the BBC dropped him
from commentating on athletics.
Linford almost lost his job
on BBC's *Record Breakers* too.

But in 2001,
his two-year ban came to an end.
In August that year,
he won a court case against a magazine,
and helped clear his name.

Lottery money (£30,000 in all)
helped Linford get back to work
as a top coach.

One of the athletes Linford coached has said:
'He was the only British athlete
to go and take on the best sprinters
in the world.
Why does everyone put him down
in such a hurtful way?'

Linford Christie has worked hard for his success.

Linford has the answer:
'I'm no saint.
But I don't pretend to be what I'm not.
I tell it like it is.
That can get some people's backs up!'

In November 2001,
one UK newspaper asked the public:
Which British black person
do you most admire?
Which black person has done
the most for society?

Linford came second.
Only Trevor McDonald,
the ITN news reader, got more votes.

Linford Christie, OBE, MBE,
knows that success is not won easily:

'There are no short cuts,'
he tells young hopeful athletes.
'The harder you work,
the better you'll get.
Enjoy yourself. Work hard.
You'll get the results.'